28 FACTS YOU CANNOT DENY BEFORE MARRIAGE

(Let no man put asunder)

Rev. Richard Duah

Scripture quotation marked new King James Version were taken from the holy bible, copyright c 2016. All right reserved.

ISBN: 9789988537456

All right reserved under international copy right law

Content and /or cover may not be reproduced in whole or in part, in any form without the express consent of the publisher

Published 2016

By Richard Kwaku Duah (RKD) for short

P.O. BOX NK 303 NORTH KANESHIE.

EMAIL: Richardduah720@gmail.comm

CONTACT: +233 (244) 265745 / +233 (556) 963348 Visit - www.firezoneprayers.com / www.livingrockchapelint.com

TABLE OF CONTENTS:

PART ONE

FUNDAMENTAL TRUTH OF **MARRIAGE**

PART TWO

HOW TO ARREST THE OLD MARRIAGE CRIMINAL

PART FIVE

MARRIAGE VS CHILDREN, CHOOSE ALL

ACKNOWLEDGEMENT

It is not possible to write a book like this without the help of some noble people. Many special thanks to God almighty as my spiritual source of entity,

Special thanks also to Mr. Isaac Mensah our local marriage committee chairman and the entire marriage committee members, by their Names Mrs. Cecelia Ankomah, Madam Sophia Akoh, Madam Grace Koduah, and Mrs. Osei Bonsu.

In one occasion, an issue of just two and a half months as couples confronted the committee, and in the midst of that dialogue God revealed the book title "WHERE IS MY TRUE PARTNER"?

I can still not forget Janet Aba Mensah who supported me in diverse ways through those seasons of difficulties and encouraged my every bits of effort to save many marriages through this revelation from GOD. Oh Madam Janet Aba Mensah thank you.

Least but the list, I thank

Rev. Joseph Benjamin – Leading Saints Church

Bishop Michael Addofo - Peace Chapel – Ghana

Rev. Dapaah - Peace Chapel- Ghana

Elder Whenn –Ghana Apostolic church

Rev. Otoo Mensah Assemblies of God- Ghana

Elder Emmanuel Addai – zion Methodist church- Ghana

DEDICATION

I am Proud to dedicate this book to my lovely wife Mrs. Grace Duah and our two children king David Duah and Sarah Ammissah Duah.

Mrs. Grace Duah for her unconditional love, caring and comfort began open real pages of love in my life. King David Duah, his unconditional joy before my eyes continually.

My church elders and entire members; their continuous support, encouragement, prayers and love towards the publication.

INTRODUCTION

The book in your hand is a solution the whole world have neglected over ages and apparently; the conflict with the universe stands on the axle of marriage. The moment the whole world reason to solve the problem of marriage, God will solve the problems of the world.

*Marriage brings about **family** and family brings about a **nation** and nations brought about continents and finally world emerge out of it. The enemy first attacked the marriage and conquered it and from there it seems the devil has full control over marriage.*

The book in your hand is a special book with needed principles that every young adult must read before enters into marriage.

Every chapter has some unique ingredients that will bring about a transformation to everyone who reads it. Wonderful stories of people who incidentally went extra mile away for solution but to no avail.

After wonderful experience of many people; who some of them are **clergymen**, **divorce pensioners**, **marriage counselors** *and* **expects** *have contributed immensely for such awesome principles relating to marriage.*

As other books are relevant for our living; so this book is also going to affect the lives of many people desiring for good and lifetime relationships since marriage is part of the human race, because this book came about through inspiration.

Last but not the list; the whole world is at war with God because the major area affecting people's life is nothing but marriage which formally has been neglected over ages.

Matthew 19:6; *So that they are no more two, but one flesh; what therefore God did join together, let no man put asunder.*

FOREWORD

*Mr. Duah I have been friends for long, and it came not a surprise to me when I first hear of his book; Mr. Duah I knew was someone who goes about counseling people with marriage problems. I used to term him "**marriage contractor**" because always going round solving marriage problems.*

*As a collogue pastor, I became happy when the first title hit the wall book of the world; '**Wonderful tips to know before marriage**' knowing very sure of what Mr. Duah can do when it comes to solving marriage problem. I can recommend this book to the world as long as this earth remains and marriage remains.*

He supported the idea of pastors coming together under one umbrella to champion the king's kingdom business by fighting *against divisions among the ministers of God. After reading the entire book; one particular topic that touch my heart was **"Adam and Eve in the Boxing ring & The Mistakes in the Marriage Today Are My Own Mistakes"***

My final word to the world as the editor' is that, personally; I shall pass away but marriage still remains unchanged and for that matter recommend this book which is now bringing awareness to a particular areas which the world have given it a mere concern but critical for our living.

Thank you,

Yours sincere,

…………………………………..

Rev. Joseph Benjamin Ansah

[Firezone prayers & deliverance center]

PART ONE

FUNDAMENTAL TRUTH OF MARRIAGE

NUGGET: 1

BACKGROUND OF MARRIAGE

As we all know; before God had finished His fulltime business of the creation, inclusively the institution of marriage has also taken it course. Purposefully, as other creations like the earth and the entire universe are for a specific purpose; so God instituted marriage for a specific purpose.

Marriage institution is the only institution established by God; it has no size and that it stands unquestionable. It was first companionship established by GOD for Adam and Eve when Adam was alone in the Garden with animals, both living and non living creations.

Before the intensity of God's plan had actually been achieved, and also the secret this book as is going to introduce to you another levels, ironically or otherwise decided to hide or cover the sight of the man so both can cherish and respect each other. But on the more serious note; the impact fell on the man despite that the woman was taken out of him in the first place or being the same flesh.

God chloroformed Adam so he may not see anything during the operation so he may [**the impact**] also respect and cherish the woman. That is exactly why it has become a general task for every man to search before finally mine out for a woman or a wife under all circumstances up to date. (**Genesis 2:21-25**)

Every woman is a '**gold**' covered by the soil and as you and I know how difficult it is to mine for any mineral ore in the heart or bottom of the soil so is a woman. Any virtuous woman is like a precious mineral ore hidden in the soil and requires so many tools and general studies of geology before even one may set out for mining.

Man was created or forms in essence that he should never be alone neither will he be complete if he doesn't excavate hard to find out the true partner or the woman who was taken out of him. Women should also understand that they were form out of the man as his helpmate so they should also begin preparing vigilantly awaiting for that man who will also make them complete.

After the Man has successfully finds the helpmate which was taken out of him, he then becomes completely full man and from there he begins to execute his natural duties which was assign for him to accomplish; reproduction, regeneration and all the blessings that accompany him.

Few of his blessings are as follows –

Genesis 1:27 And God prepareth the man in His image; in the image of God He prepared him, a male and a female He prepared them.

Genesis 1:28 And God blesseth them, and God saith to them, **'Be fruitful**, and **multiply**, and **fill** the earth, and **subdue** it, and **rule** over fish of the sea, and over fowl of the heavens, and over every living thing that is creeping upon the earth.'

I don't want to mislead anyone about anything concerning the real meaning of marriage, since it is the oldest God made institution on earth. Many great authors in history have done great job to define inside and out of marriage; therefore over here I stand no chance of misleading anyone the true story of marriage but emphasize more on the other areas which are also going to be important to us.

It is the oldest institution by the reason that, all over the world; weather villages or towns, marriage is recognized, the outer most part where the real gospel of Christ has not been propagated, the institution of marriage is by nature and traditions or by ordinance means recognized.

Since it was the plan of God man can never through his ideological means change the system which is from **ADAMIC** age instituted; we would find it better to turn to the master planner; who when we turn to him will unfold every secret beneath the carpet,1) **Preparation**, 2) **Integration**, 3) **Continuation**, And 4) **completion**. I am still under the influence of the Holy Spirit to follow accordingly the instructions given to me concerning the procedure to which this novel should be written

Any person who tries to tarnish the original master plan or the blue print of marriage shall face rough confrontations and the bad side of God. You're warned!!!

POINTS TO BEAR IN MIND

1 Marriage is the only perfect institution on earth since is not manmade art for the reason that any other institution is manmade art and shall pass away.

2 Any perfect thing requires search, survey, longsuffering, and persistent before one can find it or mine it out.

AT THIS POINT I WANT YOU TO ASK YOURSELF THESE TWO QUESTIONS;

1 **Why do you want marry?**

2 **Are you trying to marry because it's an old tradition and therefore compulsory?**

The subsequent chapters will unfold readiness one need to know before he or she enters into an unbreakable and successful union or marriage.

NEGGET: 2

DO YOU CONSIDER MARRIAGE IN GENERAL AS A COMMAND?

A

ccording to genesis 1:26, Elohim said, lets create man in our image and after our likeness to have dominion over all that we have created....... ,these indicate that it wasn't the request from man to have wife but **GOD HIMSELF** for the following purposes- dominion, authority, reproduction, replenishment and also follow by an accountability.

Commandment always comes with accountability or punishment, for God commanded them saying; be fruitful, multiply and replenish the earth. Since God commanded them on that note judgment is likely to follow one day. Any person who tries to change or divert the original master plan for another thing or similar like homosexuals, lesbians, family planners and so forth will automatically face the rough of God.

I'm trying to draw your attention to this topic very well because the whole world has lacked maximum credibility before the creator concerning marriage. We often heed to instructions and verbal commands from fellow man, like business bosses or mistresses in our various places of work, whereby down plays every commandment from God for the reason that we don't see HIM in person. Our earthly authorities hardly take offenses lightly with us, then how much more our heavenly father who presides over all.

Marriage in general is a commandment from GOD, and every creature on this planet should simply understand that; because many people have forgotten to recognize that aspect of the commandment pronounced by God. From this very expression, I know human race is now going to adhere to this biblical commandment as important as it is.

<u>POINTS TO BEAR IN MIND</u>

1 After God had created all things, marriage was the second thing God created so when a person recognize marriage as commandment as it stands then one through a gradual process gains recognition and obedience before the creator.

2 Since marriage is the beginning of reproduction and regeneration, any

person who respect marriage has already build acceptance and companionship with God through this commandment am preaching about.

<u>AT THIS POINT I WANT YOU TO ASK YOURSELF THESE TWO QUESTIONS AS YOU'RE GOING TO ENTER INTO THE MAIN BUSINESS;</u>

1 Do you know why many people have fail in their marriage life?

2 Do you know why so many people consciously or unconsciously struggle in their marriage for survival?

NEGGET: 3

ALL INSTITUTIONS ARE NOT PERMANENT EXCEPT MARRIAGE

What God has joint together let no man put asunder' **Matthew 19:6**, is a clear understanding to us that, marriage is the only perpetual institution on earth; it has no expiring date, no moment of retirement till death do us apart.

All **manmade** institutions on our planet have expiring date and are no permanent. People usually retire from indigenous occupations and professions but history has not been able tell us an expiring date for marriage, according to the bible, couples are not allow to separate or couples to go on marriage leave as it is permitted in our professions nowadays.

Man can do more in his professional studies but we need extra miles to acquire knowledge in marriage which happens to be the longest institution on earth. It is an institution that needs enrollment from crèche, kindergarten, primary, junior high school, senior high school and even to the Tertiary level. Situation like this needs enough studies and preparation to get the person much endowed.

Ministers of today are capable and confident enough to take marriage couples through three months training or as is usually called marriage counseling and assign them for everlasting institution like marriage. It's so disgusting to discover a fact that, people of today are able to suddenly pick their partners from usual places like party grounds, hotels rooms, and funeral grounds, onboard and on public places for marriage.

The situation am talking about here is far beyond the normal attention and recognition we give to it, in fact it requires in birth or deprogramming attention. Parents on this note suppose to train the children right from childhood to be acquainted with the principles relating to marriage.

Parents must speak the language of marriage with the children, cook with it, to be like the food they eat, sing marriage songs, marriage dance, and in everything we do as human beings. The Holy Spirit deeply became real to me under this topic when HE revealed a scripture from (**PROVERBS CHAPTER 22**: **6**). Train ups the child the way he should go, and when he grows, he will not depart from it.

Marriage training is a necessity for every parent to incline to it. My dear fellow reader, just consider this fact; all over the world you and I including all have acquired knowledge through education, but there is no absolute peace in the world.

People do their best and even spend more money to acquire knowledge with the sense of making life meaningful, but the consequences are even worst. Education in general is good, but the situation where all have accepted the fact that peace and success are derive from education is where lies my argument and also why this topic under discussion is a must read topic.

A fact well understood in the world today are people of great achievement, which most of them are little or less education are however connected to favor; irrespective of their education background. Few of these great men in history are Mr. Bill Gate, Abraham Lincoln, Dr. Dr. Osei Kwame, Henry Ford, Nana K. Gyasi and Dan cote`etc.

The real principles for success in life, which mankind seems to have ignore, just consider this; bible says in the book of (**PROVERBS CHAPTER 10: 22**). It's the blessings of the lord that make rich and added no sorrow with it. Emphatically, I want to stress out that if we have something to boost of, then it should be marriage and not education because that way have failed us, the mere facts remains that when one has peace in marriage same has peace with God.

As a concern minister, I advocate and request that, marriage syllabus will one day have it way in our education setting so our children may adventure into such subject as a study from the basic level to the tertiary level, So far as marriages are concern.

Majority are the class of people who go through emotional torture because of wrong marriage partners they selected in life without much knowledge about the inside and outside of marriage.

Professors and noble men have committed suicide by hanging themselves, taking in of poisons, stubbing themselves and sometimes applying various means to take away their lives. After God has joined Adam and Eve in the garden, God said it was good because it was a **perfect match**, and then how come that now it is bad and even gotten to worst?

For the lack of knowledge my people perish **(Hosea 4:6)**, my brother my sister let's begin to admit the fact that we have failed God for not applying the knowledge HE spoke about in marriage. Frankly with you, anytime a man by virtue of select wrongly partner, you naturally confiscate your peace, joy, success, favor, greatness and finally break a divine law.

A good and a virtuous wife who can find (**proverbs31:10-31**) and that wife is worth of than a fifty (**50**) years old professor of the law school. Wrong selection of mate can lead you to your early grave. A good partner you find in life is your '**GOLD**' in the soil'

NUGGET: 4

ARE YOU NOW PREPARED ENOUGH TO MARRY?

According to **proverbs 18:22,** it reads like this; he who finds a wife finds a good thing and shall obtain favor from God. I urge you to deeply consider this one thing as you read over. Before someone tells you that if you are able to find this thing or this precious mineral happy are you- immediately what comes into your mind?

It indicates that the person is actually drawing your attention on some vital or mystery no other person can easily pick it on the floor or find. Although is an undeniable institution in the journey of man, but **GOD** is actually informing us to be more vigilant in the search for it because; all genuine doors of blessing pertain to life hangs on it.

The human manual from God keeps instructing us to prepare well with proper tools for checks and balances from all angles before one enters into marriage, because that searching mistake alone can cost you all. Marriage itself is inevitable, but at the same time an enemy of progress that one shouldn't fails to recognize it principles outlined in the bible.

Many great researchers and philosophers in history have generally confirmed that rise and fall of every man is in one way the other depends on marriage partners. It's both a disease and remedy, it builds and it breaks. Since is perpetual, I encourage every person to adhere to the ongoing principles with maximum effort and additional high level of study, vigilance, and without mistakes.

Most especially the young person's preparing to enter should remember to embark on a study journey to fully understand before their motions begins to lead them astray.

Naturally I encourage all without fear and panic to marry as the master planner encourage us in the bible, since is our anchor to God's blessings and any great status in life.

Any person who understands the rules and procedure of the game; with the necessary stuffs enters into genuine marriage and doors of blessings, respect, recognition and fame and finally becomes obedience to HIS maker.

NUGGET: 5

RIGHT TIME AND PLACE TO CHOOSE YOUR MARRIAGE PARTNER

An incident occurred in my life one day when an old man around asked me, so where **is** she? One way or the other, we all mingled with people from different walks of life, starting from the time where we started school, time where we intend to learn trades, from our various places of work, etc.

These areas are coupled with mixed sex where marriage opportunities were available to all and most especially in our basic schools; Imagine sitting in a room with collogues for nine (9) years and times go further to secondary schools and far to the university.

All this precious time in our life passed away unfruitful because the society lacked the knowledge to use such medium profitably. After wasting this marvelous opportunity, the same person graduate from school and begins out a life; then begins to search for a partner whereas those monitoring privileges were at his or her disposal, suddenly picks up a partner from the roadside for a wife or husband.

These countless opportunities begin from **Sunday schools, primary schools, and our local communities**. These three areas are very critical in this dialogue. Sunday school for instance the advantage are always there where their teachers could have taken the chance to pair them meaningfully in this principles, but woefully this moment passed by for free. Nine whole years went by in the basic school without a click on these principles and not forgotten our local communities where parents have the all chance to begin to pair the kids on these principles but also went away untouched.

Parents, teachers and pastors this is out time to start enlighten the kids right away to change the usual plan or format. To continue the story, later when I was of myself, I realize that the woman whom I have known in the church during my youthful age was my best partner.

Why, because I have known her very well, the family, her friends and relatives almost throughout my life, we were together in church activities and so much to my family and friends. I had the chance to study her dos and don'ts because the shyness was completely drove away.

God is always certain that we can't deny and do away with His instructions, God said, "train up the child the way he should go and when he grows he will not depart from it" When this topic becomes part of our tradition and portray it as culture, the children become familiar with the principles and by so doing we gradually become in birth to it. Basically, with this principles well **coded** right from the early stage of life, we reunion with the master planner and designer of marriage.

The only three recommended areas suitable to choose your partner are:

1. The local community where you were born or grew up.

2. The local school you attended.

3. The local church you were born in or attended.

I am sorry to say; when a young man neglect these three areas and look elsewhere, the tendency to flop is obviously clear.

PART TWO

HOW TO ARREST THE OLD MARRIAGE CRIMINAL

NUGGET: 6

APPLY ANTAGONISM

Antagonism in this early stage is very necessary in essence that at this moment; the reader is entering into a very crucial area where all your investigation tools are obviously required. This area is where the entire marriage problems have begun throughout over ages.

You are going to enter into a process where one would absolutely be dealing with a complete spirit entity in disguise. Why am I saying this, according to **genesis chapter 6:6**, God said it has repented HIM to create a man and continuing from the book of **Psalms 8:5** which reads this way; And causest him to lack a little of '**Godhead**', And with honour and majesty compassest him.

This book is presenting a key to your understanding why so many things went wrong in the marriage; after God had created man so many things went wrong after man had fall, to a point where God Himself said it has **repented** HIM for creating man because; though HE had created him but the ability HE gave him has resulted in ruin and for the reason that GOD made him little lower than GOD; has compel him and man still possess the ability to think to himself as God.

Am trying to bring you closer to a point where I can confirm to you that man is a complete spirit entity; and for that matter possesses enough ability to ruin or debase his fellow human being. The word antagonism I mentioned earlier is a new dimension to apply in the beginning process to identify few truths about the opponent especially in the courtship stage.

As new entries, it's very necessary to apply antagonism to help you provoke your partner in the courtship process to identify characters and emotions. The reason for this application is that we usually allow our emotions to lead the courtship process.

Out of desperation, a lot of people have jumped into conclusion instead of acquiring the necessary principles relating to marriage. Where had all this desperations had comes from – Age factors, Family pressures, Peer pressure factors, their livelihood support factors thinking that leverage will come from the partner, all their mate are ahead of them, and many other beautiful reasons.

The tool **antagonism** is very necessary because by this application one will begins to enter the process with the idea of friendship, to be able to outline the forgoing principles one by one. Basically, friends have so many things in common which indirectly exposes true characters of persons than having the marital intensions or idea only in the process.

A lot of interviews were conducted before I judge it a fact in this dialogue that all those who begin the process with the sense of only marriage normally don't prosper; but only the few who have known the secret have prospered. I can easily insult my friends with the intension of finding out truths but the same situation can never be dealt with the person in the courtship process.

I hope you're gradually capturing the difference between the two scenarios in the process. This topic alone can cover many pages but I still remain in the procedure. Dealing with your fellow human being is the most difficult situation ever on earth.

GOD, through His word said, "**Proverbs 11:30.** The fruit of the righteous *is* a tree of life; and he that winneth souls *is* wise. Because the same processes applies to win a man or woman soul as partner in the life of marriage race. For this reason the bible says he who wins a man or woman wins a good thing and obtain favor from God. (**PROVERBS 18: 22**) consider this popular quotation, "an enemy you know is far better than an angel you don't know".

Since marriage is a perpetual institution, I therefore encourage our generation to divert from the old system where people begin to court after they are too old enough or the so call three months counseling. Many people ask me; Rev. It's a nice approach, but when I begin that approach will I not provoke my propose partner to eventually quit? Or won't **I** be the looser? Assuming he/ she happen to be the right partner.

Okay my dear; if that same person through impatience becomes your worst partner what will you do also? The right partner will endure all obstacles with you till you successfully arrive at a destination. Do you also know that our emotion sometimes deceives us if we don't logically apply the necessary tools in the search? **A word to the wise is enough.**

NUGGET: 7

KNOWLEDGE FOR MARRIAGE IS VERY ESSENTIAL

Lack of knowledge my people perish is direct from the maker of marriages (**HOSEA 4:6**) according to the bible. The world has been very meaningful and worth for our living because of twenty percent people who have directed their knowledge very well. They have all done very well in the field of engineering, science, fabrics, agriculture, telecommunication, etc but the knowledge for marriage is obviously uncertain.

The secret about all these knowledge is that all shall pass away, because it's **manmade** knowledge but marriage institution shall not pass away and therefore requires higher knowledge than the craftiness of men. Before we can appreciate God we need to acquire knowledge that can sustain our marriage and there is no source than to turn to God who from the ancient of days has design institution of marriage.

Through this chapter, we identify few of them:

Knowledge about who man and woman are, dressing knowledge, speech knowledge, sex knowledge, knowledge in finance, child bearing knowledge and their upbringing, knowledge about our in-laws, knowledge in dietary etc.

You are gradually coping with me that a lot have been down played leading to disastrous and woeful marriage. All these and many more are the things we need to know before entering into the institution that is call marriage. The manual provided by the maker is the true source to secure the necessary knowledge available for perpetual institution called marriage, without throwing our weight about on God we may but, possibly unable to finish to course.

Young person's trying to know the truth of **the PAST, PRESENT AND THE FUTURE**, must adhere to such principles undergoing for integration against something we call, broken heart, cheat, divorce and separation, etc

NUGGET: 8

PSYCHOLOGY FOR MARRIAGE IS VERY ESSENTIAL

God created us in His image and after His likeness, in the image of God He created us". (**Genesis chapter 1:26**)

The psalmist also says, "He made us little lower than God" (**chapter 8:5**) do you agree with me that man is a spirit, okay lets study the background few human individuals who proved in history that man is indeed a spirit.

There was a man in the bible called Enoch who lived hundreds of years and later was taken to heaven with his body incorruptible,

Elijah was also taking up into heaven with the physical body.

 Mary the mother of Jesus also, there is an iota of truth that she disappeared and finally our master Jesus who ascended to heaven with a lot of people beholding him catching into the clouds.

Man despite everything, possesses a unique spirit in him that distinguish him from many other creature beings because man both possesses physical body and also the spirit form at the same time. It only God and man that have the ability to repent but angels and other spirit don't, indicating how unique you're among the other creatures. I gave you this mental picture for you to understand certain mysteries about the topic under discussion.

Psychology in general is the study of the part of the spirit in man; as is usually refer to as soul in most of our dictionaries. The world scholars have neglected one most important ingredient which should have long been factored into the education systems but have only reserve only for just few class of people in the society.

Psychology is not something that should reserved for only the grown up, tertiary level graduate or security personnel but in our basic level of education, so every living person will at least have insight about psychology in the race of life.

When it comes to dealings with our fellow human beings, we have no idea, no solution and strategies than to apply psychology.

The general social race is about possesses the ability to win the opponent in marriage or in business, but as you can see our attention is widely on marriage, so the content portray much more of that than business.

Since marriage is the medium to receive God's blessings or the favor He spoke about, the enemy is much more into it than any other thing found on earth.

That is why **chapter 6** of this book refers to it as old marriage criminal, so you and I may seriously consider the possibility of not allowing any mistake which would appear in the marriage. When marriage laws are broken, it's a first sign of downfall in one's life.

In fact I feel to write more on this topic under the influence of the Holy Spirit, but since is a sample, I reserve till your recommendations, and patronage and sponsorship are received before the full volume and details would be published.

NUGGET:9

MARRIAGE IS A FULL TIME BUSINESS

Men mostly spend more time in so many things which may be very important but I want to tell the world that, though all these areas might be relevant enough but time we reserve towards marriage is not enough per my research and discovery.

My research indicates that all those areas of business are complete and coupled with expiring date; but marriage has no expiring date. You could be very busy in your field of endeavor but business for marriage should be paramount. Nowadays people worship their businesses which call for no accountability neglecting their marriage business which will one day attract the rough and the judgment of God.

God has nothing to boast except marriages, which out of it the purpose of reproduction and regeneration had continue making you and I members of it. I want you to Judge this story and see if these couples had taken marriage as seriously business; such catastrophe would have happen to them. These couples had their ceremonial wedding, attended by prominent people and the marriage ended in three months later. What had caused this sudden divorce; these couples were in relationship for years and many seasons passed by with so many abortions and later on celebrated their official wedding. After the wedding something happened and here is the story which resulted to the divorce.

The woman now was of age and demanding for a baby whereas the man was also not ready at that time and this turned the whole house on fire. The man was insisting they should wait till their return from abroad but the woman was just opposite to that decision.

Not knowingly her doctor had confirm to her that another abortion could bring a fatal disaster, so out of fear of abortion per the doctor's advice the woman was insisting for a baby; and also pressure from friends and bad advice, compel her to think otherwise by stop using contraceptive so she could conceive.

This misunderstanding persisted till a friend introduced her to another male friend for adultery and after the husband had found out; the situation couldn't hold water to stand the humiliation, disgrace and rumors that was escalating everyday than to file for divorce thinking that she could be barren if she continue to stay with the same husband.

True marriage comes with all these responsibilities and I confirm it a business and not a joke. The knowledge I am talking about here is something very serious that I encourage every young person to mean it business and chase after it.

NUGGET: 10

SATAN'S CHILDREN ARE STILL IN OUR MIDST –JAZEBEL

King Solomon was fortunate to be allowed to marriage many wives, upon the privilege he had later landed him in a shrines where God was furious with him despite all his greatness, fame, recognition and kingship status. The root cause of King Solomon's predicament began when he had chosen to follow idolatrous women which are something that God hate and at the same time abomination in His sight.

According to (**genesis 4:16-18**) Cain was a son of Adam but so many incidence happened where God drove him out of the garden of Eden, but we got know that Cain knew his wife and conceived. If I may ask who was that woman he married to?

According to the bible the world generation started from over here but how come Cain got woman to marriage, and where from that woman. Do you know what, the writer is gradually by the walk of a tortoise coming closer to revelations which are over the years bordering you?

An interesting story Continues from **chapter 6: 2**, that the sons of God saw the children of men and married multiples as they could. Very shortly am trying to push you to understand that there are other children on the face of the earth who are children of men and for that matter are Satan's children. Anything that belong to Satan or for that matter come from men are questionable and also I believe that the first 'conception' was from **SATAN** and not **ADAM**.

I confirm spiritually with the bible that after Eve accepted the offer from Satan, Eve conceived with Satan since she took the fruit from the snake before Adam the true husband took his office according to **chapter 3: 1-17**. Because the end product was Cain who was rejected but Abel was accepted being from the true father.

We have so many Jezebel around whose purposes are to force young people to commit immorality and also to cause every products from them become vagabond only to be unaccepted by GOD.

We need to be watchful and vigilant in selection of marriage partners because of wolfs in sheep clothes in us; without allowing Satan to become our **in-law**. These untimely mistakes have landed many people to ditch where they are not able to return. These Jezebels are all over looking out for people to devour.

As am gradually enlightening my dear ones to be extra vigilant on how these jezebels operate, consider this fact; before Joseph was born he carried his talent and vision in life but alongside in a certain time in his life, jezebel plan to plug it out as most of us know the story.

Jezebels are vision killers and nothing else, so every young person in life preparing for marriage shouldn't take such area of awareness for granted. They only come in to still, kill and destroy as the bible has already declared. Every plan of blessing hangs on two things and these are **PEACE** and **JOY.**

Though, I still write in a nugget form; let me highlight on the two ingredients I just mention above- the **peace** *and the* ***joy***.

A lot of people are going through life difficulties because of wrong partners or jezebels they selected in the marriage journey, whereby the **perfect peace** that they suppose to enjoy; to attract the blessing from the right source becomes clustered with obscurity and eventually miss focus in life.

Naturally, one can never attract anything good because; according to law of attraction when there is no peace the waves become unclear. Remember also that when there is peace automatically the joy being the second ingredient portrays it.

In marriage, your partner is the supporting anchor so when the anchor fails you in the ocean you either drunk or you shall be beaten by the storms of life.

Since they are agents of the enemy, they tactically finish the course assign for them and after they accomplished the mission; turn away as we usually consider it to be **divorce,** which is something that **GOD** hate to hear about. I mentioned earlier that, these are the principles to consider in our various schools as syllabus so as we grow, we may be thus prepare in advance for the inside and outside of it.

Frankly speaking, the devil is not after anything **material** but your **soul** and the seed of the soul is in the marriage; so when the devil conquer the marriage he conquer the soul and the seed of the soul as well. When God created all things without marriage there was no record of temptation until the marriage institution came into being.

The world is in crises for the reason that we didn't cherish marriage institution which **GOD HIMSELF** established; which the world should have consider paramount among other things in the world's history.

NUGGET: 11

ADAM WAS OLD ABRAHAM WAS ALSO OLD

I 've personally live to observe little fact in life that is very necessary and useful and can never be avoided. So many people have undergone through this trauma and didn't come out successful because they couldn't recognize it harm in the marriage journey.

Biblically, God created Adam long before the request for the woman; and after the woman had appeared the man Adam had lived with the creatures long enough which indicate that Adam was old before Eve.

Before Adam had finished naming all the living and the non living creatures, confirms that; it was not a small journey. Abraham was ten (10) older than Sarah as we all know from the bible.

These evidence are yards stick to guide every person who under goes the process of getting marriage, for a fact that women are not just weaker vessels in decision making but also weak in the physical stature as well.

Let not your emotions overtake you when selecting opposite mates for marriage so far as age is concern. Naturally women spend their age time faster than men because of how they were created and other attributes which are also natural as per their menstrual cycles, and reproduction systems and many more. As every tree blossom with flowers and whiter away so do women by age and physical features connected to them

Am making reasonable statement over here if the world would consider these things very well, especially the religious sects. These incidents are ongoing and it goes round to affect the female partners at long rounds. Most women have made the mistakes when they realize marriage was a concern to them and by pressure from friends and families after long awaited with no results.

Women usually face the insults from the men like; you're not my class, are you a woman to be married after she had help the man to gain recognition, fame, business growth and other things in life. When they were around their youthful stages both were looking good and other stuffs.

 But well after forty (40) years the woman begun to bend down whiles the man stands erect with developing muscles. So many changes begins to occur to the woman; starting from the hair down to the toes, especially the shapes, the front and the butts with many other things in the system and around the system.

Life begins at forty where money and other things start to flourish; if the foundation had been built well. Every man has a particular eye which capture ages around 20 – 30 years.

Since the man is now of himself, the advantage and the chance of meeting high level ladies who have the initial features he found around you from the start still hovers around him and this time even worst.

The age difference is very critical for every young lady in the process of getting marriage to avoid being victim of humiliations.

NUGGET: 12

ADAM AND EVE IN THE BOXING RING

The bible is the foundation stone for every truth on this planet, but we normally consider the easy way neglecting the hard way. What is the hard way? The hard way is the search for the secrets truths in the bible, which we are bit by bit being discovering them through the principles underway.

Eve was the first person to taste the fruit and testified that it was good, and fair looking, and also good to be eaten. When Adam was innocently away, she gave him the fruit to eat and by love he didn't complain.

Am confident and convince to tell the world that women are good marriage proposers than men. Adam had long been enjoying the greener pastures in the garden over years and suddenly Eve appeared with all the charming looks every beautiful woman can boast of. They were both going about in the garden but Adam was so weak to confess his love to Eve; and because he delayed to propose, Eve had to advances the process.

After the compliments, **bone of my bones, flesh of my flesh** and he ended there over years which look so boring to Eve; women are very good in situations like this but what they lack is the procedure and the proper tools to use.

But our dialogue is gradually showing us the way to apply the proper tools and procedure to guide them properly. (**Song of Solomon 3:1- 4**) its reads; "for all night on my bed I have been longing for the man of my love, but I did not find him, I went about the streets searching for the one my heart loves.

The night petrol team found me on the street and asked me; what you're looking for you young woman! I replied; the man of my heart"

And when she find one; she bring him home to the mother for introduction. Upon this story, do you see anything wrong with the story?

In all over the world, history proves that women are the ones who usually go out in the street **'excuse me to say'** for the prostitution business, having the gad and the courage to wait for men no matter how the condition is, sometimes dangerous to hear them narrate their story, but they still stand without fear and panic to welcome any man that comes.

Women are still good proposers in the process. I conclude to the world that, Eve first broke the love protocol in the Garden of Eden and that same line could be traced back in history. Adam would have continued rubbing the chin till thy kingdom come, if Eve had not taken the initiative. Women; just apply these recipes to help you lead or advance the process to sort for your partner.

From the beginning of these principles, consider the two items mentioned earlier in chapter 5 - **time** and **place** around your own community.

1   *Sport the person you admire and be sure he is single*

2   *Trace his residence address.*

3   *Present a gift with your name and contact and short words like; do you*

know I can be a wonderful wife to you?

4 *I will call on you soon*

5 *Neatly rap the present and send it to him*

Make sure you master the principles outlined before; since they are your tools. Without them you can flop on the way

NUGGET: 13

HOW DO YOU JUDGE POLYGAMY?

Why it is that one woman is not sufficient for a man **Matthew 19:8** "He saith to them -- 'Moses for your stiffness of heart did suffer you to put away your wives, but from the beginning it hath not been so" there is not one biblical evidence that permit men of all class the right to marry more than one wife, but most men do their analyses base on the trait of king Solomon or the patriarchs.

Even if it's so, they usually forget that their not kings as they were. Do you see it wrong to inquire from your propose partner his or her opinion on polygamy before the marriage? Do people even ask?

Did you understand him when he answered **YES, NO, or NEVER?** I personally distinguish Africans by far leading; when it comes to issues relating to polygamy. Gradually the Holy Spirit is leading the way by dropping into my hunches the secrets which have been hidden from ages since creation, constituting the plagues of this world.

The Ten Commandments had all come from marriage, the commandment came to meet marriage; because the people for the and the law for the people and as you can see, the old law we couldn't comply and same applies to the new law which is Christ's law. All because the foundational pillars which is the marriage; we didn't consider those areas well, so every product from it is likely affected.

We usually quote from the bible to justify our cases base on King Solomon that he married **700** wives and **300** concubines forgotten the new testament how the savior package the same words to buttress their opinion.

Most of our African traditions allow polygamy whereby I can stand on that note to defend such ideology since is always in the interest of the men. My umbilical cords are tie to a family where polygamy is a game we play but today I am telling the world that such act is the root cause of the rough of God upon humanity.

This narration might seem furious to many readers but that will not change the course to different dimension since I know God is speaking to you through me, and confirm to you that it's a human institution and not GOD.

After God had form the woman out of the man; the man confessed saying bone of my bones, flesh of my flesh; and **GOD** confirm to them that it was good. Few errors occurred in the Old Testament which after Christ came to amend them for our own good, then why should we reflect much on the old laws.

In the preparation process, through your application of this new principles or tools- when your propose partner gives you an answer like '**YES**' in the conversation, then I urge you to begin to quit the process after series of correction are made and your opponent refuses to obey or follow suit.

When he or she answers '**NO**' it's a sign of progress but not the full answer because there is the possibility that one day when situations change for the better same partner has the chance to divert the course change his or mind. The third answer is '**NEVER**' which is correct from the series of interviews I gathered, I can speak on authority that **never** is the true answer base on the level of the communication and the application of the ongoing principles.

Don't make the mistake and enter before you make the attempt to find out or quit. Let me tell you frankly that any person with slightest dream about polygamy is a complete **thief** and I repeat with an authority.

Now consider why they are thieves; have you ever heard in history as one man at a time performing marriage rites to two women before? They all know that their in-laws will not allow that to happen or thrust their daughter to a polygamist.

It all starts one after the other; not even when they are young but after they are however well to do or little bit cushioned up financially. My young ones who are about to enter should not hesitate and shy to find out all these facts before you enter into the marriage. Anyone who doubts my analysis should try and ask from history whether people can marry two wives at the same time.

If it were to be good wont they present the two women at the same time? A word to a wise is enough.

NUGGET: 14

COURTSHIP TIME A SERIOUS TIME

One big mistake in our courtship today is the word '***PITY***'. I learned so many things when I was running an interview on people, especially with the ladies in general. Most of the people I interview nearly mentioned the same word ***pity***, which grounded me the seriousness for the day.

The ladies were eager to express their views this way; to the extent that, when the men approach them for the first time they feel embarrassed or bad to say **NO** to them or virtually by not offer them what they ask for. Naturally men hardly control themselves in situation of sexual expressions and in often time like courtship or dating and the least chance they get; they try to express their feelings in the form sexual intercourse. Over here the men becomes subjected to every request made by the women and try to spend their last money even if they will die for love; buying cars, expensive cell phones, outing, organizing parties for you, shopping, in fact over shopping etc.

Then they begin to narrate their past experiences that, they have had enough with other ladies and have decided not go into relationship anymore; ever since I broke up with …lady **A** or lady **B**........ I had never touched a woman before; I am patiently preparing to find a woman that will understand me for the rest of my life to avoid similar experience.

Over here the women begin to behave in a manner that; they have landed at the right destination by concluding that the guy might be the right partner so no way she is going to lose him.

The women being the weaker vessel they go extra miles in their dresses because of fear of not marrying to her is half way driven away, putting on attractive dresses exposing themselves half naked against a naked fire and the end result is just opposite, i.e. fornication, abortions, pre-mature pregnancies and so many unprepared marriage.

Woefully, most of the ladies narrated their stories this way- after lengthy narration, they also feel to bowl because after all she is also a woman with mindset that after being too stingy the marriage chance might also pass by without grabbing it.

And before they realized what actually make up their women hood has been giving or express for the lowest price ever; things have been too late than ever. But bear in mind that the upright judge of all things is not respecter of persons. God put a veil before every woman no matter what circumstances you're, weather educated or not, rich or poor, big or small, class or no class- a special covering that makes you a virgin naturally.

This spiritual veil makes you a virgin and moreover reserved for the rightful partner to usher you to your "**SECRET ALTER**" as the holy matrimony to the bed undefiled. But they ignorantly stand on the platform called *pity* to finally defile themselves with different men or women forgotten the master judge.

 But HE will also punish you bitterly for not recognizing HIM as the master planner and therefore deserve the best honor and recognition from the wonderful institution he established. **In the moment of courtship, pity not each other.**

NUGGET: 15

DO YOU KNOW THAT MOST LOVES ARE COUNTERFEIT?

People usually buy dresses with the idea that it will fit or look fine on them; but later if they don't look nice in the dress they either dash it out or stop wearing them. Secondary we try to match every dress with its shoes or sandals. God gave Adam the perfect match thus Eve; every pair of trousers goes with a particular shirt, ladies usually dress according to accessories that match the dress.

Every cooking wear has its lid or cover, buildings are designed to match the roof and that is the general rule in life. Majority classes of people are going through frustrations in their marriage because they didn't consider the kind of mate that match with them. Most of the marriages today are not true marriage; but what I have termed **counterfeit love.** I later realized that people can never be trusted, and especially women and few of the men. Ask me why?

It dares me to find out the truth by interviewing masses on this subject whether we have what we truly call counterfeit love or not; and the discovery was a phenomenon and more disguising. Truly most of the marriages today are under the impart of counterfeit love or love mismatch.

Most ladies I interviewed on this subject disclose to my attention that; though they in marriage but with wrong partners due to many reasons at the time. The true love was not prevailing, but peer pressure, age frustrations, financial reasons, traveling opportunities, education support, family funeral support, birthday party support and other things have landed them there,

The marriage proposal and the acceptance came by the back door through joy and later realized they were not the perfect match for them. So later when the marriage circumstances had begun; there were no other ways than to look for or file for divorce in the long run.

Do you know why all these circumstances had happened, then let me tell you why; they lacked one principal tool called **psycho** plus **knowledge** for the marriage? That is exactly why this book is gradually preparing us on the way for the future.

In fact those items mentioned above which have landed many in disaster are very fatal to our marriage success and as such very rough on our way. Because the two parties did not match, it becomes very obscure to their blessing doors as far as the cosmos force exists.

The two parties by slow poison encounter disunity, disloyalty, misunderstanding, grudges, struggles, quarries and one secret thing is insult within; insult like you are not my class, by mistake I got married to you etc. It's so dangerous to marry someone you don't love.

There is this secret in life that 'if one doesn't love, he hates'. According to the universal law of marriage relationship,

When a situation like this happens, its only one out of ten that can stand the heat of divorce.

NUGGET: 16

THE RIGHT TIME TO PROPOSE MARRIAGE

I am not surprised you are asking **WHY** this topic at this time about the word *'PROPOSE'*! Upon my series of investigations, this word proposes was paramount and generally challenging, mostly to the new partners preparing to enter into marriage.

Let me share with you a little story of my past around 1998, where I was active and a young Christian; how this word *"propose"* saved my life from a Christian sister. The story goes like this; we were three brothers to two sisters in the youth ministry.

Among the two I became too acquainted with one of the sisters to extend that; the entire youth ministry assigned us a name –

the most holy singles. Upon that intimacy, and the level of teasing we received from friends, no option than to cope with them and agree to prepare my mind towards her for marriage. Just a pooper and beginner in life, empty financially and almost in everything; all because I was just around 20 years of age and also inexperienced in matters relating to marriage.

Because I was financially unstable I delayed in the process of delivering my message of **'propose'** to the lady for a long time but all indications show that I love her even to the altar. Both families agreed to merge with us since nothing seems to separate us; but something happens which turn my story around.

Among the other two brothers; one of them decided to consciously or unconsciously take away what belongs to me. Through this agony, I realized men sometimes stab their fellow human beings throughout of emotional torture, how come a close friend may turn all of a sudden to love his friend's lover.

The pain persisted for a long time until one day I gathered the courage to organize a meeting with her to solve the situation once and for all.

Through that meeting the truth came out; and there lies the truth, this my lady friend told me plainly that, "**Richie as she used to address me – you and I have been friends for a very long time but you've not even one day made an attempt to propose love message to me before but your friend did and I saw the seriousness in it and I also accepted the proposal**".

Quite unfortunately, this brother friend didn't take her anywhere and they couldn't marry, over the years later she got married to another man full of troubles and humiliations engulfed them till they finally parted; but later when she came to her senses, I was also then married.

Later I realized that she was the impatient type which a lot of people carry them as a challenge on their part. A Youngman who having heard my narration asked me; rev. won't I be the loser if I delay to propose love to her? With the fear that someone will just go ahead to propose or snatch her leaving me in the dust?

Listen for good why this book is your book so you and I can recommend it to everyone who desires good and acceptable marriage and also our reunion with the **MAKER**. This is for a fact that; a woman weather young or old haven hears the word **propose**; turns to be a different person altogether.

They begin to change the attitude towards you making sure that all the **odds** a shape well for the better, because that word **PROPOSES** is the only word behind the veil between male counterpart and the female counterpart.

For proof and evidence, I traveled to another village in Ghana and stay there for six months, and over there I decided to try my plan if it will work out. So after two weeks of my stay, I met a lady who for a reason commenced my plans towards and wonderfully the plan worked out.

After pretending this way; amazingly she asked me only one question, are you not married, You men of today; if you're in only for friendship and not marriage just back out.

After hearing my flattering words she just understood the point where I was coming from because I courageously **PROPOSED** to her about marriage. In this *'propose'* process, I want you to act like a criminal investigation officer, (C I O) so you can gradually identify reasons why many marriages have collapsed.

Many people, I mean almost all hesitate during this period of engagement, and **propose** their mind to the opponent which mostly goes to the men in the process. Women for certain are very particular about the word **PROPOSE** and this for sure has landed many into misery. What helped out of my story was the delay which brought the **impatient** habit in her out.

PART THREE

MY ROLE TO PLAY

IN THE

MARRIAGE

COURSE

NUGGET: 17

HOW PREPARED ARE YOU TOWARDS MARRIAGE?

{Who am I?}

The principles under part three of this novel are very crucial and challenging and are separate topics on their own but being my first book I ask for my dear readers' comments, recommendations, and support for the complete publication hereafter.

Each topic contains vital elements which in this our age are very important for every young person desiring to enjoy a successful marriage to read; however, all are going to appear in the form of questions you may ask yourself. Try to be transparent and truthful by asking yourself those questions whereas you wait patiently for the next edition.

<u>**IT ALL GOES LIKE THIS:**</u>

WHEN YOU ARE ANGRY WHAT DO YOU NORMALLY DO?

DO I KNOW MY ETHICS AND CULTURE?

DO I PARTICIPATE IN SOCIACIALISM?

DO I COUNT GOD AS THE FIRST CAUSE?

AM I THE MOST EXPRESSIVE TYPE?

AM I THE MOST CARING TYPE?

DO I DEMAND TOO MUCH?

AM I THE MOST TRANSPARENT TYPE?

AM I THE MOST FASHION TYPE?

AM I THE MOST GENEROUS TYPE?

AM I THE BEST COOK TYPE?

AM I THE MOST HYGIENE TYPE?

AM I THE MOST RESPECTFUL TYPE?

AM I THE SEXIEST TYPE?

AM I THE MOST OVER SPENDING TYPE?

AM I THE JOYFUL TYPE?

AM I THE MOST RESPONSIBLE TYPE?

AM I THE TIME CONSCIOUS TYPE?

AM I THE INDUSTRIOUS TYPE?

AM I THE MOST CREATIVE TYPE?

AM I THE MOST ECONOMICAL TYPE?

AM I THE MOST LOVABLE TYPE?

AM I THE MOST RELIGIUOS TYPE?

CAN 50 - 70 PERCENT CHARACTER ENOUGH TO MEET THE REQUIREMENT?

CAN I AVOID SEXUAL SELFISHNESS

HAVE I CONSIDER THAT PRAYER AND FAITH BURNS ALL BARRIERS?

DO I ALWAYS APPRECIATE GOD?

After answering all these questions best to your satisfaction; a lot of things will begin to happen in your life about marriage that will bring many surprises to you, because those are the very challenging issues that put many back from their marriage. That's is exactly why I called them wonderful principles you must know or read before marriage.

PART FOUR

BANTAM WEIGHT

STAGE

[SUSTAINANCE]

NUGGET: 18

MY RELIABLE ANCHOR

From the early chapters we have been updated that marriage is the only perpetual institution on earth, perfectly designed by the creator Himself for general purposes which are all beneficial to mankind.

This part of the book is going to emphasize much on couples after the marriage, and other areas which are also much necessary and a guide tool to sustain the marriage; more also for people who have mistakenly entered and are facing challenges.

What they need to do to sustain the marriage and season it to have a new facelift. **Proverbs 18:22** *Whoso* findeth a wife findeth a good *thing*, and obtaineth favor of the LORD, It indicates how hard it is to find a wife; because of its hard implications, it requires hard work, wisdom, knowledge, psychology, intelligence, persistence before one can **'find'** the good wife.

Every **precious ore** requires certain apparatus before they are mined out and the same applies to finding a vitreous wife. Every man desire for success and advancement in life but as well as I know, is impossible without the help of a vitreous woman.

According to the generally accepted rule or quote, behind every successful man there is in quote a **'woman'**. The principles are just divine inspiration and not something that we can formulate or could be traced from a particular source. Dear reader and a friend I want to encourage you to consider them carefully for your good.

Great authors of the age have marriage encyclopedias and novels but actual solutions to marriage challenges have never been found, since from King Solomon's age till now as if marriage problems are normal.

But I want to tell the world that this book will be a marriage book for you and the future generations.

Favor, in general, is almost the same as grace and its only good and successful marriage that attracts and unlock that beautiful gate of favor or grace, not the hard work; according to (**Proverbs 10:22**) The blessing of the LORD, it maketh rich, and he addeth no sorrow with it. [KJV]

You and I are very good judges over people who fortunately had gotten the privilege whether consciously or unconsciously fished out the right rib; [partner] how all things also work together for them. You may bear me witness that; those couples seem to be on the side of God whereas others are in the dust as if God hates them.

Before we move to the real spices under marriage sustenance, may I draw your attention to those who by mistake have taken to themselves wrong partners how miserably they are beaten by the challenges and storms of life? Everything seems to be falling apart like the **titanic.** *Your life anchor is your very partner in life; that is why God classified them as helpmates.*

NUGGET: 19

PARENTS; DON'T BREAK THE HOME

Many broken homes today are due to parents who neglected their responsibilities; which resulted in **separations** and eventually **divorce**. When parents entertain any member of the two items mentioned above, their children are not far from a school dropout, teenage pregnancies, and one neutral secret that occur to the children are the following- aside from the bitterness, misery, pain, they naturally begin to develop hatred towards other parents and their children who have watched carefully against any of the members being under discussion.

How do I conclude that to my dear readers, children all over the world are innocent in as much as they were on a distant planet before this; excuse me to say, **irresponsible** couples decided to bring them into another planet known to them as earth.

 The three necessities we all know; the shelter, the food and clothes, the total mold of these children are under the custody of these irresponsible parents; so having separated or divorced, the control of these children becomes open to visualize any unwanted goods passing around them.

Because other parents have thus been responsible, these children begin to compare the good status of that family and draw so many things; which unfortunately they have lost on their side as a family.

Since they are under the tendency to attract anything passing by, the enemy who is behind all these perpetrations from the Adamic age begins to expose these children to negative s0ituations like armed robberies, criminals, occultisms, prostitution, tricksters, betrayals and different religious beliefs or sect.

Gradually envies escalate through them as they grow within that neighborhood towards that responsible family for the peace, unity, togetherness, success, modalities, good education, sustainable job or work; their way of marriage and so on they have toiled for and are enjoying.

Parents who mistakenly allow this incidence to happen are on the wanted list of God for bringing innocent children to the world to be treated like this, thus by handed them over to the evil one.

This awful situation of divorce is widely spreading globally as if all human efforts are completely unable to find solutions to divorce situations.

One awful unconsidered thing that happens after divorce in our world is that the victims become a mockery in society; either party loses self-esteem, fingers will be pointing at you and others think that you have certain bad characters; that is why men or woman can't marry to you.

I encourage that the last thing one may think of doing in life is to consider what is termed as separation or divorce. Aside from being evil in the sight of God, don't even try to be on His wanting list at all.

Even marriage cases that have reached the verge of seeking legal advice for divorce; I can assure you that after reading this book, we shall say no to such cases of divorce in our life after this enlightens.

Since these whole ongoing topics are about couples, I give my general advice to all couples to rush and get copies of this book and begin to adhere to the principles which through inspiration have been outlined by the author; to reinstate and straighten every crooked ways which has befall them in their marriages.

Don't let divorce take you to hell but you take it to hell.

NUGGET: 20

YOUR CHILDREN ARE YOUR PERMANENT INVESTMENT

Proverbs 22:6 Train up a child in the way he should go, even when he is old he will not depart from it.

Parents invest in your offsprings for this is right. There are so many areas that parents can invest in their children. Education for instance, is one major key area that when parents invest their wards; will later turn to be gold; when parents in this way begin to impart knowledge as the Holy Bible has directed everyone to do; the foundation becomes solid as a rock.

Proverbs 9:10 The fear of the LORD *is* the beginning of wisdom: and the knowledge of the holy *is* understanding.   Parents, who understand what life is about, usher their children to the right source, and the right place available is a sound religion.

When the parents begin this area of investment at the right time of their life, it yields fruits at the age when you are between 50- 60 years where your strength and ability are begun to fall down or far spent. Then your children take over from you the baton and reduce stress and hard work.

Every parent desire that their children grow to become a particular person in life as clergymen, state governor, business director, sector minister, doctors, mechanical, farmer, actor& actress, musician, and so on; will depend on the kind of investment you invest in the child.

God knew that HE has blessed you with everything that you need to train your offsprings to become whom you want them to be. Your children will become who they are base on the positive instruction they receive from the right source, likewise negative instructions will shape them accordingly.

Most parents don't recognize this aspect of responsibility at the right time and now their guilty conscience is at war with them; making them feel irresponsible and embarrassed among the society. Few areas which have to render them irresponsible parents had come from the time where their energy was at its peak **i.e.** most of such irresponsible parents had spent all their resources in an unnecessary and sophisticated lives like expensive phones, exclusive cars, unconcern funerals, extreme budgets, over affordable apartments, over expensive schools for their wards and unnecessary show-offs.

I quiet remember a story of two neighbors who were arguing and comparing over their children's school; teasing each other over the amount they pay per term per child accusing the other of poor tuition and other stuffs, forgetting that all fingers are not equal so also shall all class never be equal in life.

Life is a journey and not an easy journey to be able to predict the future or its destination today might be very sweet but tomorrow might be very rough or bitter; so parents should be mindful of persistent savings toward the future and their children investment portfolios.

Proverbs 10:5 He that gathereth in summer *is* a wise son: *but* he that sleepeth in harvest *is* a son that causeth shame.

Systematically when parents follow the various principles this book is gradually introducing, and apply them to life, God almighty will surely consider the situation and our marriage will take its new form and our God would be rejoicing over our marriage one day.

NUGGET: 21

DON'T FIGHT A GHOST- FIGHT A GOAL

Many people try hard to fight **GHOST** instead of **GOALS;** why? Every human individual is a complete entity created by God. Everything GOD created was good and has been good till now and will always be good forever. So who are we and our wisdom to comment on it? No one is perfect as this book taught us that character marginal line is 50 -70% and just accept it as a pass mark.

Fighting a ghost is simply means **misunderstanding** in this dialogue; so many couples are going through trauma because of fear being harbored in them for no reason. Don't forget that you were alone as a complete entity before marriage joined the two of you together with as one, however; the features that makeup you are still the same in the marriage.

The 50 – 70% attitudinal set-out or otherwise mentioned earlier is describing every character that made up you, for you to understand that no one is perfect so as you join to your partner; and therefore may not expect your partner to be 100% in character wise.

Kindly consider this phenomenon as you read over, there are 26 alphabetical letters which each stands on their own – the same letters when they are joined together, the same letters begin to behave differently.

ALPHABETICAL LETTER **'H' alone is impotent**

'U' alone is impotent

'S' alone is impotent

'B' alone is impotent

'A' alone is impotent

'N' alone is impotent

'D' alone is impotent

That is {husband}

Now let again consider how the same words begin to formulate when their fellow counterpart are joined to them rightly or wrongly.

ALPHABETICAL LETTER [*wrong categories first*]

'**F**' + ool = fool

'**B**' + ad = bad

'**S**' + tupid = stupid

'**I**' + diot = idiot

'**W**' + rong = wrong

ALPHABETICAL LETTER [*right categories*]

'**F**' + emale = female

'**H**' + usband = husband

'**S**' + weety = sweety

'**F**' + lesh = flesh

'**W**' + ife = wife.

There was nothing like couples until two separate entities came together before we had what we can now call couples. God said, for this marriage reasons; therefore shall a man leave his father and his mother, and shall cleave unto his wife: and they shall be one flesh. (Gen 2:24 KJV)

There is a clear indication that two whole entities from different backgrounds with different behaviors and characters are now coming to merge as one flesh. Before this mixture agrees to get uniformity, it's not a day's journey or job.

There is this word **misunderstanding** that I would want to express it little over to my dear readers, how it has ruined so many people in life. Now consider this story which happened to these couples in their marriage to the extent of landing them in divorce.

These couples had successfully been in their marriage for over 17 years praying to God always for favor and blessings; and their answers were heard and heart desires were miraculously granted. Now joy was at the fullest, they change the environment, their wards were transferred to another school, and not quite long the man bought a car and a set of furniture to furnish their new apartment.

Because of change of environment; those new neighbors were awesome of their tremendous blessings and begun suspecting the source of their income. The place of business now distanced from the usual place so as he droves car every day without his neighbors exactly knowing what he does has coupled many confusions on their mind.

because lack of transparency between them as couples; the wife began to believe the mere rumors of the people around. At one night she woke the man up for a question about the sudden change that has brought about the transformation. There were these rumors that, maybe he trades in white powder or cocaine; as they usually called it.

The wife with all humility asks the husband, my dear; please I want to ask you a question; probably if you are into drugs? Is there anything that you're hiding from me?

Immediately the husband retorted!! What are you implying of me; me into drugs, he quickly jumped off the bed with the voice up raising insults at her vigorously.

The woman humbly knelt and said I am sorry my dear with no harm I asked you that – the speculations were all over so the man has also been hearing those rumors but with no bases or facts. He also concluded that the wife has connived with the people on their views and speculations.

With pain and agony, without patience begin packing her belongings out of the house with no pieces of slightest understanding, thinking that the wife has betrayed him to the neighbors. Before the man had understood the whole truth about the story; separation had already occurred.

The family sort to settle and bring them together again but it didn't work out well for them because the woman also revealed a secret that the husband is the impatience type ever since they got married so now that she is out marriage bondage she preferred a divorce.

Now let me arrived at the causes so you don't become victim one day. From all my research as a private marriage counselor, I have derived so many causes to support my proof. All the causes come like this, **am suspecting that …….., I am hearing……..., I am thinking……….., I want to ask………., I want to know and want to find out and so forth.**

All these words are impotent until some words are added to them as I tried to illustrate them with the alphabet above. Couples who allow any of these suspecting sentences to gain grounds in their marriage, excuse me to say are cowards and inexperience in this wise and are not far from divorce.

Misunderstanding in this context is simply means - **miss sentences** between two parties revolving to grudges and has not reach a common understanding. Couples though are from different background must not tolerate the phrase describe above. Couples have become one flesh because God wants them to see each other in a mirror. Any change in the course of the marriage must be transparent to each other financially, in business, estates, education, childbearing, and all so we can both prevent misunderstanding.

NUGGET: 22

MY QUARTER FINALS STAGE

Last but not least revelation to my favorite readers of this book is to keep these questions in mind as they read over. There is this proverb in our language that says ["*the longest journey in life is the marriage journey"] as I stated also earlier, marriage is the only permanent institution on earth"* 1. **{did I fully understand every questions and answers that came up from my propose marriage partner during our courtship?}**

I made mention earlier in one of the nuggets that "we are all spirits entities in disguise"

Psalm 8:5 And causest him to lack a little of Godhead, And with honor and majesty compassest him.

Don't also forget that, we study something that Satan's children are still in our midst. You and I fully know that saying something is much easier than putting it into practices or action, best say '***easier say than done***' my dear reader am trying to bring to your attention on these mysteries in marriage, most especially our young ones who are now coming up to continue the same undeniable journey of man.

2. {Who are the right people to do the marriage vows; the new couples, the officiating minister, the persons present, or who?} This is what I am trying to bring to board from the parties who committed initially at this stage of the process. When one reaches the age of marriage, relationship, or in love; the same person is subject to challenges that are likely to influence him or control him or her to accept anything around him or her.

Weather from the right source or not and over here the male counterpart takes advantage to flatter the opponent with all manner of compliments and stuffs just to make sure he wins the opponent – the female counterpart.

At this very juncture, I write to the ladies or the female counterparts to be open-minded and not close minds to able to consider these questions and try to be satisfied with every bit of words that comes up in the discourse.

The first question goes like this

1. Why did you choose to marry me among many beautiful ladies in this city my dear?

2. Are you sure you will not dump me along the way when you're full of yourself honey?

3. Do you know that what we are planning to do is perpetual and therefore requires a deeper understanding?

4. Are you sure you're not just flattering my interest for the sake that I am in need marriage, peer pressure, family pressure, and pressure from my friends?

5. Do you know that God will not forgive us if we both commit or divorce?

Since you are acting as an investigator, you need not be afraid nor be dismay because everything is about your future and for your good.

When all these questions come to light you shall be amazed to know the kind of person you're engaged to go into **bonds** with. You shall be surprised to discover every bit of truth about your partner and that will help you to know whether he or she came in as a wolf or sheep.

All these hidden mysteries are now at your disposal to help you to prevent or escape every shock which normally results in broken heart, unhappiness, despair, separation, and eventually divorce.

NUGGET: 23

THE MISTAKES IN THE MARRIAGE ARE MY OWN MISTAKES- WHY ASK WHY?

People hardly admit their mistakes since from the time of Adam. He was in charge of the garden long before Eve joined him; knowing all the loopholes, length, and breadth of the garden, inside and out before the arrival of Eve. When the adversarial fashioned his weapons against them purposely to woefully overthrown their office - after the devil has successfully defeated them, their master; **GOD** came to them and inquire where the fault had come from.

Instead; Adam pushed the blame to Eve and she also pushed it to the snake, finally the snake would also push the blame because it was God who created it; believing that because Adam would begin to blame God for creating the snake. These circles have ever continued throughout all generations unsolved or half detected.

The mistakes that are occurring today in the marriage are my own mistakes; over here lots of people ask me why Rev. Duah, and so is you out there asking the same question why? But I am happy they eventually agree with me over my answers and there we are; upon my general survey and search, I conclude that almost all by far missed the process along the way.

Generally, the world is like a market front where everyone comes in to shop for human beings either male or female, and after having found one; decide to carry it home or any place available but our case at hand has more to do with the home. **People are displayed in many manners in** *dresses, in beauty, by sizes, small or big, by height, by education, by names, by fame, by status, by intelligence, by culture, by financial background, by cities and towns, and many more.*

When the time came for you to choose and buy these displayed items, actually nobody pushed or forced you to buy the unwanted goods home. One thing I am suggesting to all is that the goods display at the market can't speak for themselves but by their beautiful display, we are attracted to buy them. All the people you see around are like the goods display in the market; they can only attract but they can't talk, till you make a sign or whisper to the seller or the controller and ask for the price before possibly buy them.

Kindly ask this question and move along – *how did your partner came your way?* You see the picture; he or she didn't call you but you did the call. Now compare the market scenario and see if there is some difference in what I am saying. On the more serious note the ladies in this context can vividly see but they can't talk but they do wait patiently for a call from the men to buy them and carry them away.

After calling them you give them the audacity to talk back or ask why you called them, so in the situation of human beings, we both have the legibility to express our views whenever necessary in a context like this. Most of the goods we brought home have an expiring date on them already which begins to generates an effect on us, others are not expiring dates per se but are either oversizes or in size, and so on.

However, I may suggest that the keys [**principles**] which we should be familiar with were out of the scene; so in the case of searching for a partner in marriage, one stands in position like the goods displayed in the market place. Our motions diverted the course by taking the lead so before we realized, the real tools to put in place for the good findings have been either misused or were found wanting.

It's a big mistake to accept marriage proposals that come your way without first doing your very best to apply the recommended **tools** or follow the **principles outlined**. Any bad purchase you make towards your marriage will result in pain, agony, misery, frustrations, bitterness, barrenness, witch hunting, force religion, and the end products of wayward children to be produced in our society.

Having brought my points to the board they began to bear with me that my points are unique and it stands no other, before agreeing with me that "the mistakes in the marriage today are their own mistakes. In conclusion, I recommend that the youth of today will take advantage to prepare their way with these principles to escape the deceptions of Satan.

NUGGET: 24

DO YOU KNOW THAT SATAN HAS WIFE AND CHILDREN WITH US?

Dear parents, you carry bigger responsibility to make sure your children get married early in their lives proofing from the bible root because God supports early marriage.

Adam did a big mistake in the garden after Eve had appeared by delaying much time allowing Satan to advance the purpose of marriage by consummating Eve through the marriage right.

Genesis 3:1 And the serpent hath been subtle above every beast of the field which Jehovah God hath made, and he saith unto the woman, 'Is it true that God hath said, Ye, do not eat of every tree of the garden?

Because the bible says Satan was subtle; Adam shouldn't have wasted much time in his advancement, paving way for Satan to sleep with Eve. I know that majority will agitate on my expression and I know you are also asking; if its true weather Satan had sexual intercourse with Eve.

God created man with a certain distinctive manner that; he can never look on a woman without first something striking through in his emotions or shocks of thunder striking through him naturally. When Adam saw Eve so many things ignited in him by complimenting Eve with all manner of words.

Genesis 2:23 and the man saith, 'This *is* the *proper* step! Bone of my bone, and flesh of my flesh!' for this it is called Woman, for from a man hath this been taken;

Just imagine Adam and Eve always walking about naked in the garden with Eve carrying all these beautiful eyes catching looks with her, the butt, the hips, the breast, the hair, the neck, the thighs, the eye, the nose and many more; in fact; the first female creation of God.

Satan being canning and crafty realize; that Adam had no idea about making love to the woman; so Satan tried to step up possibly to show them the use and before Satan had realized he has rather been attracted to what doesn't belongs to him because of how Eve was going about naked in the garden and how attractive she was. Satan though being an angel; couldn't control himself as you also sometimes can control yourself.

By Satan seducing the woman to love him as we usually refer to as the fruit, something happened and that is exactly what I am almost about to narrate to you soon than later.

After all, these things had happened; our first mother Eve had a conception and bare a son, and they called his name Cain and now let me tell you this, Satan has children with us because the son Cain belongs to Satan since he had caused the first conception, there had been a controversy between Adam and Satan over Cain and their descendant till now. Satan knew for sure he is the father of Cain.

According to Genesis 4:1 And the man knew Eve his wife, and she conceiveth and beareth Cain, and saith, 'I have gotten a man by Jehovah;' literally it is true that Adam knew his wife and bare him a son but spiritually Satan had caused the conception before Adam, Satan being the biological father decided to take possession of what belongs to him.

I know that many have already begun their argument over this statement because it's appearing new to many people; but that is a fact I am narrating to you. Because Cain; was not the right son from Adam, his offering was rejected; but Abel's offering was accepted for the reason that he was the right son from Adam.

Also, consider this; **Genesis 4:17** and Cain knoweth his wife, and she conceiveth, and beareth Enoch; and he is building a city, and he calleth the name of the city, according to the name of his son -- Enoch. Cain being the first of Adam, where had he gotten the wife in the first place, so you can see I am making a point here base on the reference I am making.

Genesis 6:2. That **the sons of God** saw the daughters of men that they were fair; and they took them wives of all which they chose. Over here the story goes on to us that there two groups of people on the earth at that time.

The sons of God and daughters of men; under which generation had the other group come from since there was only one generation from the beginning, Adam's generation only. Where Cain did got a wife to marry- since there was no other generation; because there were no other people on the face of the earth.
If one group happens to be the sons of God then the other groups of people belong to which generation or from where?

Cain belongs to Satan as his biological father and daughters of men are female angels who cooperated with Satan to accomplish a demonic agenda against men and these are the children I am referring to as Satan's children.

Abel was accepted because he had come from the right channel and therefore regarded as the true generation of Adam. Not forgotten this point also, my office as Rev. Minister; many people come with their regular struggles with spiritual beings in their dreams having an affair with them to the extent of seeing physical expressions.

Men nowadays have double marriages, spiritually and physically; which creates a lot of challenges in their marriages which most of such men go through financial and job unsustainabilities.

Going forth, I want you to check out this as we ascend to the conclusion, **Romans 1:24** wherefore also God did give them up, in the desires of their hearts, to uncleanness, to dishonor their bodies among themselves;

 Romans 1:25 who did change the truth of God into a falsehood, and did honor and serve the creature rather than the Creator, who is blessed to the ages. Amen

Romans 1:26 Because of this did God give them up to dishonorable affections, for even their females did change the natural use into that against nature;

Romans 1:27 and in like manner also the males having left the natural use of the female, did burn in their longing toward one another; males with males working shame, and the recompense of their error that was fit, in themselves receiving.

 Romans 1:28 And, according as they did not approve of having God in knowledge,

God gave them up to a disapproved mind, to do the things not seemly;

Romans 1:29 having been filled with all unrighteousness, whoredom, wickedness, covetousness, malice; full of envy, murder, strife, deceit, evil dispositions; whisperers,

Romans 1:30 evil-speakers, God-haters, insulting, proud, boasters, inventors of evil things, disobedient to parents

Romans 1:31 unintelligent, faithless, without natural affection, implacable, unmerciful;

Romans 1:32 who the righteous judgment of God having known -- that those practicing such things are worthy of death -- not only do them, but also have delight with those practicing them.

I am revealing this secret to my dear readers and the world at large; so men can also understand why the world conflicts with Satan because he is our rival from the beginning of the system of things.

So my dear young ones, don't just get yourself a partner without first considering all these facts available to you but prepare very well by applying these principles in good use.

PART FIVE

MARRIAGE VS CHILDREN, CHOOSE ALL

NUGGET: 25

CHILDREN, DON'T BETRAY YOUR PARENTS

There is yet another secret I will reveal through this book about our children in line with marriage. Many marriages are collapsed beyond repairs all because of their children. However; other marriages axle also stands on the children who I think is scripture fulfilling and is in order.

Children all over the world must understand that before they were allowed into the world by their parents, the parents were in harmony with whatever they do as couples.

Most youth of today are in the center of the marriage as deciders or referees officiating for both parties spiritually and physically.

Remember that before you arrived, your parents were one flesh according to the bible; in love, peace, they understand each other at all levels before they planned of your conception and arrival.

So many things happened in your upbringing; after feeding on the breast for a year and over, began to crawl on the ground; till the time you started walking, carrying you to school, washing your clothes more than three times a week, teaching you how to speak, spending all their monies on your education, feeding you three times a day, not considering shelter and more that I cannot mention all at once.

Your parents couldn't enjoy to the fullest all because of you, building a house of their choice delayed just because all their attention was on your upbringing so you can secure a be fitful future in life and that intention had crippled them and their marriage till you are grown up to well control status.

You were not alone, but your junior ones were also consistently arriving increasing the economic hardships on them from bad to worse.

 After all these struggles and life challenges finally arrive at around 50 years thereabout deducting from their life span of 70 years, then you turn to reward them with betrayal, insults, disrespectful, backbiting and so on

Some of the youth today is ingratitude, trying always to separate their parents by conspiring with one to attack the other and this mostly occurred through the women to make sure the father loses respect in his own family. This nervousness gradually sock the man's blood till finally takes him to his early grave.

Just consider how the conspiracy is done to the fathers in the marriage; because the women are mostly close to the children often, they begin to share the property while the man is still alive convincing the children to possess what he or she thinks will benefit them when the father is no more.

I quite remember a story while I was in the city of Accra –Ghana, there I learned that a particular tribe; it is mandated for the children to inherit from the father's side. A man just our next neighbor encountered similar case from the older son by telling the father to move out of the house he built himself because he is the son; he stays in his father's house.

The son because of this narration harasses the father anytime he is drunk and this situation continued till I witness the man's funeral and burial. Others attack the parents spiritually through other means I mentioned earlier concerning spiritual entities that are mingled with us in this world in the means of the strongmen bible mentioned their names in Galatians.

Galatians 5:19 -21 [LYT] And manifests also are the works of the flesh, which are: Adultery, whoredom, uncleanness, lasciviousness, idolatry, witchcraft, hatred, strifes, emulations, wraths, rivalries, dissensions, sects, envying, murders, drunkennesses, revellings, and such like, of which I tell you before, as I also said before, that those doing such things the reign of God shall not inherit.

A child of today can tell a parent that I can see you are not my mother or father for the reason that he is being corrected from something the parent think it will not end up well for him or her; at times referring the parents of not furthering his or her education after he refuses to adhere to their instructions. Others forgot how far they are being brought from for not aborting them entirely.

1 Timothy 4:12 – 16 [LYT] let no one despise thy youth, but a pattern become thou of those believing in word, in behavior, in love, in spirit, in faith, in purity; till I come, give heed to the reading, to the exhortation, to the teaching; be not careless of the gift in thee, that was given thee through prophecy, with laying on of the hands of the eldership; of these things be careful; in these things be, that thy advancement may be manifest in all things; take heed to thyself, and the teaching; remain in them, for this thing doing, both thyself thou shalt save, and those hearing thee.

Proverbs 19:18 [LYT] Chastise thy son, for there is hope, And to put him to death lift not up thy soul.

Ephesians 6:1 – 3 [LYT] the children! Obey your parents in the Lord, for this, is righteous: honor thy father and mother; (which is the first commandment with promise ;) 'That it may be well with thee, and thou mayest live a long time upon the land.'

My dear ones don't happen to be the victim of divorce or separation and not forget that God will not forgive all who offend their parents in this way.

NUGGET: 26

PARENTS, WHO IS YOUR CAIN AND WHO IS YOUR ABEL?

Have live to analyze few things in life which are very critical but are not considered in the human race. Though the power of reproduction is in the hands of mankind but the creator presides over them all. So many tragedies are befalling the world today because of the areas we have both neglected as parents and are also affecting our generation.

According to the book of john; **Genesis 3:16** for God did so love the world, that His Son -- the only begotten -- He gave, that everyone who is believing in him may not perish, but may have life age-during.

God didn't love part of the world, leaving the others, but He did love all; but what do we see today, **Discrimination**, **separation**, and **isolation** on the side of the parents. Division is a product of Satan which many parents don't know and not just a mere product but being driven by strong forces of Satan.

Genesis 37:3 And Israel hath loved Joseph more than any of his sons, for he *is* a son of his old age, and hath made for him a long coat. The moment father Jacob exhibited that extreme love towards Joseph, the product I am talking naturally emerges among his brothers to the extent of killing him.

So who had caused that hatred among the children? Though father Jacob might not have any bad intention about the initiative probably on his mind; but the outward expression spoke to his sons on that matter.

According to the plan of God; the only medium that joins two parties from nowhere to become one flesh is marriage so how come parents turn to be discriminative towards their sons and daughters have forgotten that their one and that combination had produced their offspring.

This revelation made me to understand that the whole continents are in division and hatred because it was an in birth products from ourselves but have not been recognized.

If parents understand that they are one; discrimination would be a thing of the past and therefore will unify every product or their children as one person on the globe.

Other parents consider some of their children more potential than others, picking those as their **ABEL** whereby rejecting the others as their **CAIN**. I was so glad when I discovered that, every mistake that occurs to our children is something that we neglected to do right but failed. And what is this secret all about; is the way we intend to program the children's mind at the right time.

God made me understand that HE did program Adam's software perfectly on his hard disk for him and afterward we were given the mandate to program our children's own. Apart from Satan being able to enter through your territory to manipulate your children, any occurrences are utilizing your negligence and improper coding or installation of their software apps.

Why am I saying this? My research led me to discover few things that human effort has never been able to achieve concerning the formation of the mind; the human hard disk is plain [**the brain**] and empty at birth till the parents decide to put software programs on the hard disk.

The software program installation has been the problem over here, this area many have failed to install relevant programs which direct the steps of the child in a way and manner to go.

The wise man of ages; king Solomon stated it this way, **Proverbs 22:6** Instruct a youth about his way, Even when he is old he turneth not from it.
The errors which are notified about your ward are not his or her mistake but the mistakes of the parents in diverse ways. Parents are the shelter, protection, and refuge both spiritually and physically for their children so the enemy can never snatch or to take away what belongs to them.

Apostle John the epistle of Jesus Christ best said it this way; **John 10:10** 'the thief doth not come, except that he may steal, and kill, and destroy; I came that they may have life, and may have *it* abundantly.

The devil is identified as thief, killer and destroyer; he steals the mind by taking control over you, kills the energy that drives one and replace it with fear, sickness, finances, struggle, etc; and finally destroys your ambitions and make sure you enter into early grave which is the ultimate destination in one's life. Don't leave a vacuum in them as far as you a parent.

NUGGET: 27

WHY ALWAYS THE FIRST BORNS?

The **"firstborn"** is a separate book title which I have a reserve for the future but since I cherish my readers in high esteem, I write to you only the bulletins; hoping for your encouragement to publish other books which are also more inspirational and enrich with other things to know in our age.

Adam was the first human creation of God and therefore we can call him the firstborn of God; however, this man Adam mess up in many areas in his life which has affected the human race till now, how he neglected his manhood responsibilities to the extent of allowing rather the wife to carry out unusual responsibilities –**all because he stigmatizes with the title firstborn.**

Cain in this discourse was first after his father Adam and the same **spell** was on him; so he did all he could but was rejected and a curse was place on him for his generation to come after him.

After Adams generation, we can recall from Abraham's generation to begin from there to check our analyses; Jacob and Esau were direct twins as we all know, but a time came in their life where we recorded Esau being the firstborn exchanging his birthright to his younger brother Jacob for food and bringing him to point of abatement or slavery before his brother.

Lo and behold, our father Isaac was about to descend to his grave where he made some pronouncement on his children concerning their future the things that may befall them and now see what happened; because Esau was also carrying the **'firstborn stigmatization'** which is under discussion, he sold out his prominent estate in exchange for food; [Genesis ***chapter 27]***

Because generation goes on, at the time Jacob was also old he called out his children and began to bless them of their future.

Genesis 49:3 Reuben! My first-born thou, my power, and beginning of my strength, the abundance of exaltation, and the abundance of strength;

Over here you can see that Reuben, was first to Jacob something happens in the life of Reuben which fulfills the discretion I am making over here. **Genesis 35:22** and it cometh to pass in Israel's dwelling in that land, that Reuben goeth, and lieth with

Bilhah his father's concubine; and Israel heareth.

How had that happen to Reuben and not any other; there is a spell on the firstborn which can never be forgotten. Abel was accepted but Cain was rejected, Jacob was accepted but Esau was rejected, Reuben defaulted and received curse— why always the firstborn.

Matthew 7:5 Hypocrite, cast out first the beam out of thine own eye, and then thou shalt see clearly to cast out the mote out of thy brother's eye.

First of all, I would like to start something from my own family probably before I proceed to another or elsewhere, my grandmother gave birth to five and my mum was the first; my mum encountered marital challenges to the extent that, younger ones after she had almost all married, childbearing also became a struggle before fortunately she had gotten three of us and immediately after my birth my dad passed away in the early 1932.

 She used to trades as a petty trader and just imagine a single parent of three children around that time in Africa. My senior brother also a firstborn to my mum and **still single** at the age of almost around fifty [50] years and life is still a blow to him without defining the root cause.

My direct first cousins who are also first to my aunties are however going through life challenges as if God is far distant from them, always complaining and struggling with life.

I am still in my family; my big brother performs very ugly in social expressions and does well when alone, very argumentative, and easily gets nervous by oppositions. He hardly turns on to modernism but more familiar to old fashions or the old school ways. After observing my family traits very well with evidence, I decided to pursue a feather by interviewing people from other tribes and it was a phenomenon.

Almost every home have similar experiences with the firstborn, relatively, the envies recorded in Jacob's children are quite not a distant away. As you read this book, consider your family' s generation and see if possibly you can find evidence to the very subject underwriting because the search was extensively conducted with a proof.

According to the quote from **Genesis 49**; we realize the firstborn is however the opener of the womb, Reuben! My first-born thou, my power, and beginning of my strength, the abundance of exaltation, and the abundance of strength;

The firstborn carries certain uniqueness or possesses different favor, blessings, special energy, ability, and other good stuff in life but most of them by majority end up in pain, misery, unfulfilling, mediocrity, and abatement in the society.

I asked why these befall the firstborn until research and discovery brought me near the answer which might also be relevant to you and the world at large.

Every mother was once a girl, and this is the very reason am yet to reveal to the world; **the yet to become a mother is new to antenatal and postpartum or postnatal, first time to receive new baby, new to the bathing of the child, new to breastfeeding, new to handle a baby and new in everything.** On this note; the new mother usually allows an experienced mother, old ladies, to do the necessities for the new mother before she learns many things in that order.

Bear in mind I mentioned earlier that human beings are all spirits and therefore possesses other spiritual abilities to do good and also to destroy; **Matthew 2:1-2** Now when Jesus was born in Bethlehem of Judaea in the days of Herod the king, behold, there came wise men from the east to Jerusalem, Saying, Where is he that is born King of the Jews? For we have '***seen his star***' in the east, and are come to worship him.

Most of these people we trust at this time are somehow; consciously or unconsciously, are spiritually very wicked and a lot of things do happen to the newly born babies which the majority of the people are not aware of anything. They see the brighten star of the child as I did mentioned earlier on this topic **[genesis 49:3]**

Around this time the child's protection emerges from the parents so when their religious state is unstable, these forces am talking about influences the child's star and if possible replace good for bad.

Secondary, because of the parent's inexperience in that new postpartum environment, they try their best to spoil the child with many unnecessary things which are not needed in the child's upbringing; forgotten to train the child with proper training they deserve, thinking that the child in this context is a king to them in that manner.

In most cases, the third child however is luckier to carry the blessings of his elder brother or the second. I pray you to consider the situation now around your family and see if truly I'm making sense over here.

My dear one reading this book; are you first or third to your parents? Check out yourself and compare it to your brothers or sisters if you could make some distinctiveness to yourself. **Why always the firstborn?**

NUGGET: 28

WILL YOU AGREE WITH ME THAT YOUR PARTNER SHOULD BE YOUR BEST FRIEND?

There is a saying that; 'show me your friend and I will show you your character' after many years of marriage experience, I decided to follow this trend to come out best on this subject.

Your best friend should be your marriage partner; the only reliable anchor in your life is your partner as I mentioned earlier under the topic, my reliable anchor; confirming that all may fail you but the only person you can trust at this time is no other than your marriage partner.

One thing to bear in mind as you're about to enter into marriage is to consider your partner as your friend. Most of the marital challenges today are however; emerge from outside friends into the marriage.

In the beginning; God join Adam and Eve and made them one flesh, which consolidates their union as couples-confirming a level of confidentialities between these parties. In marriage; there is always a secret between the two, but here is the case where we allow or neglect this portion in the marriage and allow third parties to enter.

Most of these third parties are normally singles, and over here I stress much on the female parties.

How can you share your secrets with the unmarried person; what do you expect will come out from that third party, such inexperience and immature person has nothing to give; probably attack you indirectly. Remember I told you that we are all spirits in disguise; that third party is either naïve or probably stigmatize with a particular negative character which has led to that singleness or delay in marriage.

The moment such person comes your way in the marriage; it's a first sign of disclosing or breaking the confidentiality between the first two partners, there is a saying in our language that "if a pooper promises you a cloth, first ask her name" such third party is empty, single, inexperience and immature; so how can such a person or friend naturally advise on matters relating to marriage, honestly they are empty. 'Couples are for couples and single for singles; then how come are now vice versa.

Reasons, why you must cherish your partner as a unique person and a friend, are base on these tips; I want you to consider the

right of the third party to your marriage in these areas; your marriage partner shares a bed with you but the third party doesn't, ailment care, emotional desire, financial support and more extensively about your spiritual backing since your partner is one flesh with you.

The third-party has not the right to do certain things for you spiritually and physically and very opposing agents to you spiritually. Your partner is your best friend because, even your mother cannot officially perform certain duties in the marriage but your partner does.

Automatically, your partner becomes your direct mother, sister, best adviser, physical comforter, and your life helpmate. So when one understands these few principles in the marriage; your partner gets confined in you and the original maker of marriages rejoices over the marriage.

ABOUT THE AUTHOR

Richard Duah is a minister for living rock chapel;

Richard was born in Ghana in a small town then called SINPAH in the central region of Ghana, on 5th July 1978; to Mr. and Mrs. Godfred Duah. My father is now in the blessed memory immediately after two years I was born; single parent of three around the 70s as a kenkey seller.

The only privilege I had was my elementary education; and from there I manage myself to learn a trade while still a teenager, I became a breadwinner just to support my mother and the other two.

Because of my early struggle I became an employer at the field where I had my training for almost 15 years. Rev. Duah is married to Ohenmaa Grace with one boy, King David Duah. [Alias daddy k]

Someone would then ask; how come now a ravened minister? Oh yes of your much concern my dear reader; I dedicated myself to GOD for His service because I was looking for solutions to address the constant challenges that confront our church as secretary to the marriage committee; I pleaded vigorously with God for answers and my call came surprisingly to all as minister for God with the help of my pastor friend. Upon this note; I had to dissolve the other hand so I can concentrate on this new office to accomplish the call as a rev. minister and more particularly, addressing challenges, and problems that struggles with marriage.

JUST FORGIVE MY UGLY EXPRESSIONS

Language is very deep; and most especially foreign language. I wish I can express my views in my dialect but for the sake of global benefit, I manage to write my views in a globally accepted language which I might not be able to do as my own. Concentrate more on the points I am making in this book, and not on the punctuations, conjunctions, Sentences, and grammar.

OTHER BOOKS

1. THE PENTECOST OF OUR TIME
2. WHO TAUGHT WHO/ AND WHO TEACHES WHO?
3. THE EYE OF GOD ON THE CHURCH AND MINISTRY.
4. NATURAL ENEMY AGAINST COUPLES SUCCESS.